Anti Inflammatory Diet
[Second Edition]

The Best Anti Inflammatory Foods and Anti Inflammatory Diet to Keep You Healthy

Jennifer Sather

Copyright © 2013 Jennifer Sather
All rights reserved.

Table of Contents

INTRODUCTION 1
    Inflammation Problems 1
    Why Go On an Anti Inflammatory Diet? 2

THE ANTI INFLAMMATION DIET 4

TIPS FOR COOKING AND EATING RIGHT WHEN ON THE ANTI INFLAMMATORY DIET 8

ARE YOU COOKING RIGHT? 12

DELICIOUS ANTI INFLAMMATORY RECIPES 15
    Baked Teriyaki Chicken 16
    Polynesian Chicken 19
    Turkey Tenderloins 21
    Turkey Curry 23
    Noodle-Free Turkey Lasagna 26
    Black Bean Huevos Rancheros 29
    Quinoa Breakfast Cereal 31
    Hearty Bean Dinner 33
    Quinoa and Black Beans 36
    Meaty Beans and Rice 39
    Lentil Soup 42
    Chicken and Lentils 45
    Curried Lentils 48
    Maple-Flavored Salmon 51
    Grilled Salmon 53
    Baked Garlic Salmon 56
    Salmon Ceviche 58
    Mixed Veggie Salad 60
    Grilled Chicken Cranberry Spinach Salad 62
    Delicious Cucumber Salad 64
    Tofu Salad 66
    Tofu Scramble 68

Baked Tofu 71
Lime and Cilantro Tofu 73
Tofu Watercress Salad 75
Fruit Salad 77
Healthy Oatmeal 79
Banana Nut Breakfast Cereal 81
Arugula Salad 84
Artichoke and Chicken Pasta 86
Baked Flounder 88
Black Bean Hummus 90
Broccoli and Shells Skillet 92
Chilled Tomato Soup 94
Garbanzo Bean Humus 96
Italian Chicken and Cherry Peppers 97
Mediterranean Fish Packets 100
Mediterranean Mackerel 102
Mediterranean Style Baked Potatoes 103
Mushroom Omelet 104
Roasted Asparagus Dish 106
Simple Tomato Salad 108
Spanish Chicken and Rice 109
Spanish Tapas 111
Spicy Hummus 112
Tomato and Couscous Salad 113
White Bean Soup 115

Introduction

An anti inflammatory diet is highly recommended for those that have health problems, as food can cause inflammation that will make the problems worsen. The truth is that chronic inflammation is actually the cause of a number of diseases, such as cancer, Alzheimer's, and heart disorders. Avoiding foods that cause inflammation is important, but the many natural anti inflammatory foods that you can find in this book will help you to eat healthy and avoid inflammation. You'll find that you can protect your body easily, all by eating the right foods!

Inflammation Problems

You notice swelling when it's on the outside of your body, such as when you injure yourself or you strain your muscles. You'll see the swelling, and it will cause you pain. You'll usually take steps to deal with that swelling, such as by applying ice or using heat to treat the problem.

When it's on the inside, it will take a lot more for you to

notice the swelling problems. You won't usually feel the inflammation unless it is very bad, and by then there's usually something seriously wrong. You'll have no idea if there isn't serious inflammation, at least not until your problem has gotten out of control. Whether it's swelling caused by arthritis, cancer, or heart disorders, you want to avoid that inflammation as much as possible.

Why Go On an Anti Inflammatory Diet?

The truth is inflammation is a natural response within the body. It is a means of self-repair and protection. However, there are times when this process gets out of hand and inflammation causes health issues. One of the largest health issues from inflammation is arthritis. So many people suffer with this causing the need for such an anti inflammatory diet. However, arthritis is just one of many health conditions directly affected by inflammation within the tissues and joints.

Nutrition is one of the best ways to treat any health issue and should always be the first line of treatment or defense. The foods we eat directly affect all the systems in the body, including our defense mechanism. This is what causes inflammation. If we eat the right foods it is like receiving good doses of the very nutrients that are like natural medicine to the body. And likewise, if we eat the wrong foods it is like receiving poison that will work to do harm. If you think about it, some foods are poison. They may not do harm right away, but with continued consumption the body will react negatively to it.

Eat foods that help to promote a strong immune system. If the immune system is strong, it is able to fend off illnesses, germs, and free radicals. The best foods are the foods that occur naturally with no need of manmade chemicals or artificial ingredients or processed to the point they lose their nutrition. The recipes within this cookbook contain natural ingredients. The anti inflammatory diet very closely resembles the diet the Mediterranean region consumes. You will find Mediterranean inspired dishes, which are filled with the very foods that help to treat and alleviate inflammation.

As always, seek the advice of your health care provider before starting any new diet program. This is to insure you will be okay with the diet and exercises you choose. Often medications may react with certain foods, to prevent this you need to go over your medications with your choice of diet plan and any exercise plan you may have.

The Anti Inflammation Diet

The anti inflammation diet isn't a weight loss diet, but it's one that is designed to help you keep your inflammation under control. The anti inflammatory diet menu is filled with top anti inflammatory foods that will help to prevent swelling. Some of the best anti inflammatory foods include:

- **Fish --** Most fish contains Omega-3 fatty acids, which are excellent at fighting swelling. You'll find that salmon is one of the best foods to eat if you want to prevent swelling, making it top on the list of anti inflammatory foods.

- **Olive Oil --** Extra virgin olive oil should be included in all anti inflammatory diets, as the healthy unsaturated fats in the oil will help to fight off infection at its source. It will also protect your heart, so it's a healthy choice for anyone!

- **Kelp --** Kelp and other forms of seaweed are loaded with fiber, but it will also help to fight off swelling. It's rich in antioxidants, meaning that it will be a useful tool in the fight against cancer.

- **Blueberries --** These little berries are storehouses of nutrients, and they are known for being rich in antioxidants. They will help to fight off swelling, and they can help to prevent problems like dementia and cancer.

- **Crunchy Greens --** If it crunches and it's green, it's one of the best anti inflammatory diet foods for you to eat. Cruciferous vegetables contain more than just fiber, but they all have nutrients like antioxidants, folic acid, and vitamins to help prevent swelling.

- **Sweet Potatoes --** These tubers are one of the best natural anti inflammatories around, as they are loaded with the nutrients that your body needs to fight the swelling. These nutrients include beta-carotene, Vitamin B6, and manganese.

- **Garlic --** The aromatic cloves of garlic deserve their place in anti inflammatory diet recipes, as they're loaded with allicin, sulfur, and other minerals and antioxidants that are excellent at fighting swelling in your body.

- **Ginger and Turmeric --** These two spices are loaded with nutrients, and both of them will help to prevent swelling in the body.

- **Green Tea --** The antioxidants in the tea make this your beverage of choice for your anti inflammatory menu, and you'll find that there are many delicious ways that you can prepare this swelling-preventing tea!

What foods should you stay away from while on you anti inflammatory diet?

- Sugar, refined sugar, processed syrups, artificial sweetener. Use natural honey, molasses, and the natural sugar found in fruits to add sweetness to your food.

- Trans fats, saturated fats, cheap cooking oils, oils that have a high saturated fat content, peanut butter, margarine, most vegetable oils, and partially hydrogenated oil.

- **Alcohol.**

- Dairy products such as milk, sweetened yoghurts, full fat cheese, and cream. Some natural yoghurts are acceptable, and kefir is a good alternative.

- Meats from animals that are fed grain and corn, animals that have had fat injected, and red meat. You can eat very lean meat no more than once a week, but try and eat more poultry, fish, and legumes.

- White rice, white flour, noodles, pastries, baked goods, and any refined grains.

- Artificial ingredients, with MSG and Aspartame being at the top of the list of foods to avoid.

- Foods that cause allergic reactions. If you are allergic to foods, the allergic reaction will include swelling, which can be fatal if the swelling occurs in your throat or lungs.

Tips for Cooking and Eating Right When on the Anti Inflammatory Diet

If you're going to try the anti inflammatory diet and follow the list of anti inflammatory foods, it's important that you know how to cook. Eating right is more than just avoiding putting the wrong foods into your meals, but it's about know how to prepare the food. Here are some things you need to know about cooking and eating the right way while on the anti-inflammatory diet:

- **Make It Easy --** If you're going to be trying this diet, there are limits to what you can eat. You should try and make it as easy on yourself as possible, and you can do so by buying a variety of foods to prepare. Make sure that your diet has as much fresh food as possible, as that is the food that will be healthiest and reduce your risk of inflammation. Cut processed and artificial foods out of your diet, and make sure that you buy only the raw, healthy ingredients. Focus on eating more fruits and vegetables, and your diet will succeed!

- **How Many Calories? --** Do you know how many

calories you need to eat in order to be healthy? The average adult male needs to consume about 2,400 calories per day, while the average female needs to consume more like 1,900. The smaller you are and the less activity you do, the fewer calories you need to eat. You shouldn't have to worry about gaining weight while on this diet if you eat right, so make it a habit to eat the right number of calories in your day. Make sure that you're getting carbs, protein, and healthy fats at each meal, and you shouldn't have to worry about inflammation!

- **Watch the Carbs --** Carbohydrates are both very important and very potentially dangerous. They are the nutrients that usually lead to inflammation, especially the simple carbs found in refined, white, sugary, and processed foods. Make sure that your diet includes no more than 200 to 300 grams of carbs per day, and try to make most of those carbs healthy complex carbs from whole grains, fruits, and veggies. Your food should all be low on the Glycemic Index, and should be as free of sugar and syrup as possible. You will be only eating foods that are whole or all-natural, but you still need to watch how many carbs you eat every day.

- **Be Careful with Fats --** Red meat contains fats, as do vegetable oils, dairy products, baked goods, and many other things that you're cutting out of your diet. However, remember that fat comes in all forms, so be careful even while on the anti inflammatory diet. Stay away from the oils that have high saturated fat content, and stick with the healthier oils like sesame, peanut, and olive oil. Make sure to eat lots of nuts, fish, and avocadoes -- all of which are loaded with healthy fats that will prevent inflammation. Remove the skin from any chicken or turkey that you eat, and find the meats that are as lean and fat-free as possible.

- **Protein is Important --** While on the anti-inflammatory diet, protein is one of the most important nutrients that you can eat. You're going to be cutting way back on carbs and fat, so you'll need to keep your body healthy by loading it with healthy proteins. Proteins like fish, tuna, and legumes are your best options, but chicken, turkey, and even lean meat can be part of your diet. You shouldn't eat more than 120 grams of protein per day, and make it lean and natural proteins as much as possible. Vegetable protein from beans and tofu are your best option to stay healthy while on this anti inflammatory diet.

- **Load the Fiber --** Seeing as you are trying to flush all of the inflammation-causing nutrients out of your body, it's in your best interest to speed up the flushing process. There are few nutrients that are as effective at getting rid of toxins and inflammation-causing chemicals as fiber, which comes from legumes, whole grains, and raw foods. Your best option is to eat as much of these foods as possible, as they will contain the nutrients that will keep your body healthy while you're trying to get rid of the unhealthy toxins and chemicals that are causing problems. You need to get at least 40 grams of fiber in your diet per day, so eat more fiber-rich foods while on the anti inflammatory diet for the best results!

- **Get Lots of Nutrients --** You need vitamins and minerals, as well as fatty acids and antioxidants. You can get these nutrients from all manner of places, though fruits and vegetables are some of the best sources. Carrots contain Vitamin A, citrus fruits contain Vitamin C, avocadoes contain Vitamin E, and berries, green tea, and red grapes contain healthy antioxidants. Make sure to get enough of the nutrients to stay healthy while on the anti inflammatory diet.

Are You Cooking Right?

If you're cooking, you may be using more oil than you realize. If you're going to try this healthy diet, it's important that you cook the right way. Here are some cooking methods to stick with while on the anti inflammatory diet:

- **Poaching** -- Cooking your food in water instead of oil may seem like a bad idea, but your food will come out just as tasty if you poach it correctly. You can use chicken broth to make the food taste better, and you'll find that soup base makes a great liquid for poaching. It will help your food to be healthier, and it will be equally delicious.

- **Baking** -- Baking is the best way to keep your oil consumption limited. You don't actually need oil to bake food, but a bit of fat helps to keep the food tasty. Use olive or sesame oils for baking, and make sure that your food is in the center of the baking tray in order to enable air to circulate around the food. If you marinate the food before baking it, it will be juicy and moist. You can also use tin foil to cover the baked food, as it will trap the liquid inside the food.

- **Stir-Frying** -- If you're going to cook your food

with oil, you should use the stir-frying method made popular in China. The food doesn't sit in the oil - which stimulates the production of trans fats - but it will be just as tasty. The food doesn't absorb a lot of oil, and it will be much healthier.

- **Steaming --** For vegetables, steaming is the best way to go. You won't have to do more than place the veggies in a steamer to get them to come out just right, and you can enjoy lightly-cooked veggies within minutes. Just make sure not to overcook them, as that will leech the nutrients out of the veggies.

- **Grilling/Broiling --**One of the best things about broiling and grilling your food is that it will not require any oil, but the natural juices in the food will make it tasty. Grilling is ideal if you have a grill, but a broiler is like a grill in the oven for those who don't have an easy-to-use grill. You will find far less fat in your food, and it will be a whole lot tastier!

It's very important that you avoid deep frying, frying, and microwaving your food. Boiling will leech the nutrients out of the food, unless you're making a soup that will utilize the water in which it was boiled. Make sure to cook the right way, and your food will be a whole lot healthier!

Now that you know what to eat and what not to eat - as well as how and how not to cook your food - you're ready to get started with the many recipes for your anti inflammatory diet!

Good luck, and happy eating!

Delicious Anti Inflammatory Recipes

Baked Teriyaki Chicken

This delicious dish will be perfect when served for dinner, and you'll find that it will be an absolutely delightful meal to enjoy any day of the week!

Ingredients:

For this dish, you will need:

Two chicken breasts
1 tablespoon of cornstarch
Water
Soy sauce
Orange juice
Rice or apple cider vinegar
Garlic
Fresh ginger root
Black pepper
1 cup of brown rice

Preparation:

To begin, chop two cloves of garlic into very small pieces, dicing it as finely as possible. Place a large skillet on the stove to heat, and pour a tablespoon of sesame oil into the pan. Once the sesame oil is hot, add the garlic into the bottom of the skillet, and cook for a minute - until the garlic begins to turn golden.

Drop the rice into the skillet, and cook the rice until it starts showing signs of toasting. Pour in 2 cups of water, and let it cook with the lid on. The rice will usually take about 35 minutes to cook properly, but check it occasionally to ensure that it doesn't burn.

As the rice is cooking, slice the chicken breast into four pieces. Rub the pieces of chicken breast with a little bit of salt and black pepper, and place them in a baking tray. Heat the oven to 350 F.

In a saucepan on the side, combine 3 tablespoons of orange juice with ½ cup of soy sauce and ¼ cup of vinegar. Apple cider vinegar will make the sauce a bit sweeter. Stir until the liquid is hot and nearly boiling, and drop the tablespoon of cornstarch into the pan. Stir for a minute, and turn off the heat.

Chop 4 cloves of garlic and about one tablespoon of fresh ginger root, and use the chopped aromatics to rub down the chicken once again. Pour the sauce over the chicken, ensuring that all of the breasts are covered equally.

Place the chicken in the oven, and let it cook for at least 15 minutes. Check to ensure that the chicken is properly cooked by inserting a knife. Make sure that the chicken is properly cooked, and that there is no raw meat in the center of the breast.

Serve the chicken on a bed of brown rice, and enjoy!

Polynesian Chicken

This fascinating recipe combines savory chicken with sweet fruit, and it will be a unique dish that will make your mouth water.

Ingredients:

For this dish, you will need:

3 chicken legs and thighs
1 peach
¼ pineapple
1 bunch of grapes
Salt and pepper, to taste
Garlic
Sesame oil

Preparation:

To begin, remove the skin from the chicken. Cut the chicken in half, separating the legs from the thighs.

Turn the oven on, and let it heat to 350 F.

Dice the peach, pineapple, and grapes, and squeeze 1 orange and 1 lemon into the bowl of fruit to add some sweet flavor.

Dice the garlic very finely, and use it along with the salt and pepper to rub down the chicken. Add sesame oil to season the chicken, and place them in a baking tray. Top with the fruits, and place the chicken into the oven.

Give the chicken about 45 minutes to cook, as you will want to turn the heat down to about 325 F in order to avoid burning the fruits. Make sure the chicken is completely cooked by inserting a fork into the thickest part of the chicken, until it touches the bone. If no blood comes out, the chicken is properly cooked.

Remove the chicken from the oven, and transfer it onto a plate. Serve with barley, couscous, quinoa, or brown rice.

Turkey Tenderloins

If you just can't stand the thought of spending all day preparing Christmas dinner, this is a quick and easy meal that you can make that will be just as tasty!

Ingredients:

For this dish, you will need:

2 pounds of turkey tenderloins
Soy sauce
Dijon mustard
Rosemary
Salt and pepper, to taste
Garlic
Onions

Preparation:

To begin, place the turkey tenderloin in sealable plastic bags.

In a bowl, combine ½ cup of soy sauce with 2 tablespoons of Dijon mustard and 4 teaspoons of crushed rosemary. Add salt and pepper as desired, and mix thoroughly. Dice the onions and garlic as finely as possible, or run them through a food processor before adding them into the mixture.

Once the sauce is properly mixed, pour some of the sauce into each bag. Shake the bag well to ensure that the liquid has coated the turkey tenderloins completely, and place the bags in the fridge.

The turkey should sit in the fridge for at least 3 or 4 hours, as that will ensure that the meat has absorbed the flavor of your marinade. You may want to give the bags a shake every hour, as that will ensure that both sides are coated with the liquid.

Preheat the oven to 350 F when you are ready to cook the turkeys. Remove the turkey tenderloins from their bags, and place them in an oven tray or broiler pan - depending on your desired doneness of the turkey. Let them broil or bake for about 25 minutes, checking to ensure that the turkey is properly cooked. Poke it with a knife to check for doneness, and the turkey will be properly cooked when the juices run clear.

Slice the turkey, and serve with the rest of your dinner.

Turkey Curry

This fantastic dish will enable you to use all those leftovers from Christmas dinner, or you can use ground turkey if you want a delicious variation on a traditional Indian dish. It may be a bit spicy, but it's guaranteed to be absolutely delightful!

Ingredients:

For this dish, you will need:

Sesame oil
Ground cinnamon
1 onion
4 cloves of garlic
Fresh ginger root
Turmeric root
Water
2 green chili peppers
1 pound of turkey meat (ground or diced turkey)
Red chili powder
Garam masala
Salt and black pepper, to taste
2 cups of brown rice

Preparation:

To begin, place the rice in a skillet to cook. You will need about 2 cups of water per cup of brown rice, but add an extra half cup to ensure that the rice doesn't turn out crunchy once it's done cooking. Place a lid on the rice, and leave it to cook for about 40 minutes.

Place another skillet on the stove to heat, and add in 2 tablespoons of sesame oil into the pan. Add half a teaspoon of cinnamon into the pan, and mix it in with the oil. When the oil gets hot, the cinnamon's scent will be released.

When you can smell the cinnamon, add the diced onions into the pan. Cook them until they are golden brown, and add the garlic in to cook for about a minute. Dice 1 tablespoon of ginger root and 1 teaspoon of turmeric root, and add them into the pan to cook with the garlic. The ginger and turmeric should cook for about three minutes in order to release all of their flavors into the food.

Once the aromatics have cooked, add ¼ cup of water into the pan. Bring the water to a boil, and let it thicken the roots. Cut the two green chilies in half, and add them into the pan. Add the turkey, a teaspoon of spicy chili powder, and ½ teaspoon of garam masala. Add another half cup of water, and place a lid on the curry as it cooks.

You will want to let the curry cook for about 10 more minutes, as that will ensure that the turkey is properly cooked. Once the mixture has thickened into a sauce, add a bit of salt and pepper for flavor. Taste the sauce, and add water to thicken it if necessary.

Serve over the brown rice, and enjoy!

Noodle-Free Turkey Lasagna

This dish will be the perfect addition to your anti inflammatory diet menu. You'll be able to enjoy the classic taste of the dish, but without having to worry about noodles, red meat, and ricotta cheese causing swelling in your body. It tastes great, but it's a lot lighter than your average lasagna.

Ingredients:

For this dish, you will need:

1 pound of ground turkey
8 large tomatoes
1 onion
5 cloves of garlic
Basil
Thyme
Oregano
6 ounces of Cottage cheese
4 zucchini
Salt and pepper, to taste

Preparation:

To begin, cut the onion in half, and add half into a pot -

along with 3 cloves of garlic. Cut the tomatoes in half, and place them in the pot to stew. The tomatoes will need to cook for about an hour, as that will soften them and make it easier to run them through your food processor.

Puree the tomatoes after an hour of cooking, and place them back into the pot to continue cooking. Add in salt and black pepper, as well as a teaspoon of fresh basil, a pinch of thyme, and a teaspoon of oregano. Stir the sauce well, and let it cook for another hour. (Add water as needed as the liquid boils down).

Once the sauce has cooked properly, remove it from the stove. Dice the other half of the onion and the two remaining garlic cloves, and place them in a skillet with a tablespoon of olive oil. Cook the aromatics until they are golden brown, and add the ground turkey into the skillet to cook. Make sure that the ground turkey has been cooked properly, and remove the skillet from the stove.

Add a bit of salt, pepper, garlic, and oregano into the cottage cheese, and use the cottage cheese. Slice the zucchini into thin strips, and place them in a baking tray - as you would lay out regular lasagna noodles.

Pour tomato sauce onto the zucchini, and scoop the

ground turkey onto the first layer. Cover with a layer of zucchini, more tomato sauce, and the cottage cheese. Continue adding layers until the tray is full, and the ingredients are all used up.

Preheat the oven to 350 F, and place the trays in the oven to bake. It will take about 20 minutes for the zucchini to cook, and you can remove the trays from the oven and serve while the lasagna is still hot!

Black Bean Huevos Rancheros

This Mexican recipe is the perfect breakfast, and you'll find that the delicious addition of black beans makes it a very healthy meal that will be surprisingly filling!

Ingredients:

For this dish, you will need:

4 eggs
2 tomatoes
1 onion
1 green chili pepper
1 cup of canned black beans
¼ pound of turkey or soy bacon
Salt and pepper, to taste

Preparation:

To begin, dice the bacon into small pieces. Place a skillet on the stove to heat, and fry the bacon in the bottom of the pan. Once the bacon is becoming crispy, add the black beans into the mix. Cook the beans until the liquid is boiling and the beans are hot.

In a separate pan, add a tablespoon of olive oil, and

place the pan on the stove to heat. As the pan is heating, dice the onion very finely. Add the onion into the pan, and cook until golden brown.

While the onions are cooking, dice the tomatoes into small cubes. Add them into the pan, and let them cook for about 5 minutes. Add salt and black pepper, as desired.

Dice the chili pepper into very small pieces, and add it into the pan with the other ingredients. Let the chili cook until it is soft, and remove the ingredients from the pan. Return it to the stove, and add a tablespoon of olive oil once again as the pan heats.

Crack the eggs into a bowl, and beat the eggs thoroughly to combine the yolks and the whites. Pour the eggs into the pan, and cook them as scrambled eggs. Once they are properly cooked, add the tomato mixture and the black beans into the dish. Mix the eggs together with the other ingredients well, and serve with some brown flour tortillas and homemade salsa!

Quinoa Breakfast Cereal

Need a healthy, hot breakfast to get your day started off on the right foot? This delicious breakfast cereal is made with quinoa -- a low-glycemic grain that will not cause inflammation in your body. Add to that the high fiber of prunes, and you've got a breakfast for champions!

Ingredients:

For this dish, you will need:

Water
1 cup of quinoa
1 cup of prunes
1 cup of almond milk
Cinnamon
Nutmeg
Salt

Preparation:

To begin, place the quinoa in a saucepan to cook, along with a cup of water. Once the water is boiling, cover the quinoa and let it cook for about 5 more minutes - or until the grains are fairly soft. The total cooking time for the quinoa will be under 15 minutes, so keep a close eye on it.

Once the quinoa is cooked, pour in a cup of almond milk and keep the fire on low. Add in a pinch of salt, and half a teaspoon each of nutmeg and cinnamon. Remove the pits from the prunes, and add them into the quinoa to cook.

You will be able to eat the breakfast cereal once the prunes have softened, and enjoy the delicious way to start your day!

Hearty Bean Dinner

This is a wonderful dish to make on a budget, and you'll find that it will be a filling meal that will be surprisingly cheap. If you want to save money and still eat well, this is definitely the dish you should try!

Ingredients:

For this dish, you will need:

2 cups of dried beans
Water
1 onion
1 clove of garlic
1 stalk of celery
1 potato
3 tomatoes
½ pound of soy or turkey bacon
1 tablespoon of honey
1 bunch of cilantro
Salt
Mustard powder
Oregano
Black pepper, to taste

Preparation:

To begin, place the dried beans in a large pot to cook, and add about 4 cups of water for every cup of beans. Drop the onion, the head of garlic, the celery stalk, and the potato into the water -- leaving them whole and unpeeled.

Set the pot on the stove to cook, and let the beans boil for about 3 hours. You'll want to add a bit of salt into the beans as they cook, and let them cook until the skin of the beans will crack when you blow on them.

Once the beans have cooked properly, use a ladle to fish out the onion, garlic, potato, and celery. Throw these into the garbage, as they will have absorbed all of the gas from the beans -- but will have released their flavors into the legumes.

Dice the tomatoes into cubes, and add them into the beans. Pour 3 cups of hot water into the beans, along with a tablespoon of salt and black pepper each. Place the beans back on the stove, and let them cook.

As the beans continue cooking, place a skillet on the stove for the bacon. Cook the bacon in the pan until it is golden brown, and add it into the beans -- along with any oil that is produced by the bacon.

Add the cilantro into the pot, and use a teaspoon of mustard powder and oregano each to add flavor to the beans. Let them cook until you can smell the variety of flavors, and let the beans boil for a few minutes to ensure that they absorb all of the delicious tastes.

Serve while hot.

Quinoa and Black Beans

If you want a healthy, low fat meal to enjoy while on your anti inflammatory diet, this is definitely a dish for you to enjoy! It will have almost no effect on your blood sugar levels, as both quinoa and black beans are low GL foods. It is a delicious meal that will fill you up easily and quickly!

Ingredients:

For this dish, you will need:

Sesame oil
1 onion
5 cloves of garlic
1 cup of quinoa
Cumin
Cayenne pepper
Salt and pepper
2 ears of corn
1 can of black beans
Fresh cilantro

Preparation:

To begin, place the quinoa in a pot with water, and place

the pot on the stove to cook. You'll need about a cup of water per cup of quinoa, but add a bit extra water just to be safe. The quinoa will take about 15 minutes to cook on medium heat, so keep a close eye on it.

Place the ears of corn in a pot, and add enough water to cover the corn. Bring the pot to a boil, and cook until the corn is soft. Remove the corn from the pot, run them under cold water to cool them down, and use a knife to remove the kernels of corn from the cob. Place the corn kernels in a bowl and set them aside.

Place a skillet on the stove to heat, and add a tablespoon of olive oil into the pan. Dice the onion and garlic very finely, and add them into the stove to cook as well. Cook them until they are golden brown, and add the quinoa into the pan to cook as well. Mix the quinoa well to ensure that the flavors of the garlic and onions are absorbed into the grain.

Once the quinoa has been stirred into the aromatics well, add a teaspoon of cumin and ½ teaspoon of cayenne pepper. Add the black beans and the ears of corn, as well as half a bunch of cilantro -- chopped before adding, of course.

Mix the ingredients together well, let them cook for a

few more minutes, and serve while hot.

Meaty Beans and Rice

This dish is guaranteed to have your kids begging for more, even if beans aren't their favorite food. It's a recipe that's quick and easy to make, and you'll find that the dish will be a popular one with your whole family.

Ingredients:

For this dish, you will need:

1 pound of ground turkey or chicken
1 cup of dried beans
2 onions
1 head of garlic, plus 5 cloves
1 potato
3 tomatoes
Tabasco sauce
Brown Rice
Water
Cumin
Crushed red pepper
Oregano
Salt and pepper, to taste

Preparation:

To begin, place the beans in a pot with 4 cups of water per cup of beans. Place the pot on the stove to heat, and drop 1 whole onion, 1 head of garlic, and the whole potato into the beans. This will absorb the gas, and will add the flavor into the beans.

Let the beans cook for about four hours, or until blowing on the beans will cause the skin to crack. Once they are cooked, use a ladle to scoop out the onion, garlic, and potatoes, drain the water from the beans, and return them to the stove with three cups of water added to the pot.

Dice the tomatoes into small cubes, and add them into the pot of beans. Dice half of the other onion, as well as three cloves of garlic. Add them into the pot, and let the beans cook for about half an hour more.

As the beans are cooking, place the brown rice in a pot on the stove to cook, using about 1 cup of brown rice and 2 ½ cups of water. Bring the brown rice to a boil on high heat, and turn the fire to low heat to let the rice cook until it is soft. Add more water as needed to prevent the rice from burning.

Place a skillet on the stove to heat, along with a tablespoon of olive oil. Dice the two remaining cloves of garlic, along with the remaining half onion. Cook them until they are golden brown, and add the ground meat into the pan. Brown the meat before adding a tablespoon of crushed red pepper, a teaspoon of cumin, and a teaspoon of oregano. Add salt and pepper as desired. Finish cooking the meat, and remove from the stove.

The beans should be cooked by now, so remove them from the pot they are in and pour them into a skillet on the stove. Pour in half a cup of almond milk, as well as salt and black pepper. Use a masher to mash the beans, making sure that 90% of the beans are properly mashed.

Pour the refried beans into the pan with the meat, and mix them well before serving over a bed of brown rice.

Lentil Soup

If you are feeling chilled on a cold winter day, there's nothing like a hot bowl of soup to help you warm up! This delicious soup contains all of the nutrients you need to stay healthy, and you'll find that it will be the perfect meal to eat when the weather turns chilly.

Ingredients:

For this dish, you will need:

1 cup of lentils
Olive oil
1 onion
4 cloves of garlic
2 carrots
2 celery stalks
4 large tomatoes
Salt
Black pepper
Bay leaves
Water
Fresh parsley
Paprika

Preparation:

To begin, place the lentils in a bowl, and fill the bowl with drinking water. Leave the lentils to soak in the water overnight, as that will help them to cook a lot faster - and will eliminate the gas from the legumes.

Come the next day, drain the lentils, run water over them again to rinse them out, and drain them thoroughly.

Place a soup pot on the stove, along with a couple of tablespoons of olive oil. Dice the garlic very fine, and add it into the pot. As the garlic is cooking, dice the onions to be added once the garlic has turned slightly golden. Dice the celery stalks as well, and add them once the onions have become partially translucent. Add the carrots in next, and stir fry everything in the soup pot for a few minutes.

Before you add in the lentils, drop a teaspoon of paprika, a couple of bay leaves, a tablespoon of salt, and as much pepper as you want into the onions. Sauté everything together for a few minutes, and finally add in the lentils.

Add enough water to cover the lentils completely, working with about 4 cups of water per cup of lentils.

Bring the water and lentils to a boil. Dice the tomatoes into small cubes, and add them into the boiling soup. The water will cook the tomatoes quickly, and turn it into a delicious soup. Don't forget to add the parsley before removing the soup from the stove and serving while hot.

Chicken and Lentils

If you want a unique dish that will make your mouth water and your stomach rumble, this is the one for you. You'll find that it takes a bit of work to make, but it's absolutely fantastic and an excellent choice for any occasion!

Ingredients:

For this dish, you will need:
Olive oil
2 large chicken breasts
1 onion
3 carrots
4 cloves of garlic
1 cup of lentils
Salt
Cilantro
4 tomatoes
Rosemary
Basil
Thyme
1 lemon
Black pepper, as desired

Preparation:

To begin, place the lentils in a mixing bowl, and fill the bowl with water. Leave the lentils to soak overnight, as that will eliminate the gas and make the lentils easier to cook. The following morning, drain the lentils, rinse them well, and drain them once again before setting them aside.

Place a skillet on the stove, and add a few tablespoons of olive oil into the bottom of the pan. Slice the chicken breast from the bone, and cut each breast into three pieces. Cook the pieces in the skillet, making sure that the breast is properly cooked before removing it from the fire.

Heat the skillet once again with oil, and dice the onion to add into the pan. Cook until tender, and add the diced garlic into the pan. Dice the carrot as well, and add it into the pan to cook for about 5 minutes.

Cut the tomatoes into cubes, and bring them to a boil on the stove. Cook them until they are nice and saucy, and they will turn into a thick tomato sauce.

Once the carrots have cooked, transport the aromatics into a soup pot, heat the pot, and add the lentils into the pot. Mix them around to coat them with the flavor and the oil from the aromatics, and pour 3 cups of water into the pot. Add as much salt as you want, and let the lentils cook for about 20 minutes once the water has begun to boil.

Place the chicken back in the used skillet, and continue cooking on low heat for a few more minutes. Transport the chicken into the pot with the lentils once they're cooked, and stir well to ensure the chicken is coated with the flavor.

Add the tomato sauce into the pot, as well as a teaspoon each of basil and rosemary. Let the lentils keep cooking with these added ingredients for another 5 minutes or so, and serve with a dash of lemon juice for flavor.

Curried Lentils

Nothing makes a good curry like some lentils mixed with chicken, and you'll find that this exotic dish will be just what you need to help you fill up on a healthy meal. With the addition of brown rice or quinoa to the mix, you can make a healthy, filling dinner!

Ingredients:

For this dish, you will need:
½ cup of lentils
1 can of unsweetened coconut milk
Curry paste
Salt
Water
2 chicken breasts
Quinoa
8 cloves of garlic
1 onion

Preparation:

To begin, place the lentils in a bowl, and fill the bowl with water. Place the bowl in the sink, and let the lentils soak overnight. This will make them easier to cook the next day, and will eliminate a lot of the gas. Come morning, drain the lentils, rinse them, drain them again, and set them aside.

Place the lentils in a sauce pan, and add a cup of water into the pan. Turn the heat to high, and bring the lentils to a boil. Once they are boiling, add a tablespoon of curry paste and the coconut milk. Stir well to ensure that the ingredients are mixed, and add a pinch of salt. Cover the curry with a lid, and turn the heat on low to allow the lentils to simmer gently.

In a separate skillet, add a tablespoon of olive oil. Dice 5 cloves of garlic and ¾ of the onion, and sauté them in the bottom of the skillet.

Cut the chicken breasts into small cubes, and cook them in the skillet with the aromatics. Once the chicken is nearly cooked, add it into the curry mixture and mix well. Return the lid and let the lentils continue cooking.

Place the skillet back on the stove to heat, and add a tablespoon of olive oil. Dice the remaining garlic cloves and the rest of the onion, and sauté them in the bottom of the pan. Add 1 cup of quinoa, and cook until the quinoa shows signs of becoming toasted. Add 1 ½ cups of water, and turn the heat down to medium to allow the quinoa to cook. It will take about 15 on medium heat, so make sure to watch the quinoa.

Once the quinoa is cooked, serve it onto a plate, and scoop the curried lentils on top. Add a dash of lemon for flavor, and garnish with a sprig of parsley or cilantro.

Maple-Flavored Salmon

If you're a fish lover, salmon is the best of the best! You'll find that the rich taste makes it incomparable, and the fatty acids in the fish make it excellent for preventing inflammation. This recipe will help you to make a fish that you just can't help but love!

Ingredients:

For this dish, you will need:

1 pound of salmon fillets
¼ cup of natural maple syrup (not the artificially produced kind)
Soy sauce
4 cloves of garlic
Salt
Black pepper
Fresh ginger root
1 lemon

Preparation:

To begin, combine the maple syrup in a bowl with about half a cup of soy sauce. Add in a pinch of black pepper, half a tablespoon of salt, and the minced garlic. Add half a tablespoon of chopped fresh ginger root, and a dash of lemon. Stir well to combine all of the ingredients.

Place the salmon fillets in a baking tray with a bit of olive or sesame oil coating the bottom of the tray. Preheat the oven to 350 F.

Pour the sauce over the fish fillets, and set the tray in the fridge to marinade while the oven is heating. Once the oven is hot, place the baking trays in the oven, and let the salmon cook without a cover for about 20 minutes.

The salmon will be ready to eat once it flakes when you press on it with a fork.

Grilled Salmon

If you're a fan of grilled fish, this is a recipe that you can't help but love! You'll find that it's absolutely fantastic when you make it on a wood-fire grill, but you can cook it up on the stove or a propane grill if you want. It will be just as tasty, and a lot less work to prepare!

Ingredients:

For this dish, you will need:

1 pound of salmon
Balsamic vinegar
1 lemon
Soy sauce
Salt
½ an orange
Fresh ginger root
Paprika
Black pepper
Red pepper flakes
5 cloves of garlic
3 green onions
Sesame oil
Peanut oil

Preparation:

To begin, slice the salmon into steaks. It will be easier to marinade and rub the fish if it's already sliced up.

In a bowl, combine ¼ cup each of soy sauce and balsamic vinegar with the juice from one large lemon. Add in the juice from the orange, and dice or grind the garlic and ginger very finely to add them into the mix. Add in a teaspoon each of black and crushed red pepper, paprika, and sesame oil, and as much salt as you think it needs. Dice the green onions, and add them into the mixture. Stir well to combine.

Pour the sauce over the fish, and use your hands you rub the various ingredients into the fish gently. Add a bit of peanut oil, and transfer the salmon fillets into Ziploc plastic bags. Pour the sauce into the bags, and shake to coat the fish with the liquid completely. Set the steaks in the fridge to marinade, and let them sit for about an hour as you fire up the grill.

You want the heat of the grill to be medium high, so either turn down the propane grill or wait until your wood fire has mostly burned down to red coals. Remove the salmon fillets from their bags, place them on the grill, and cook them until they are tender and flaky. Use a brush to apply some of the liquid, and they will taste heavenly once you're done!

Baked Garlic Salmon

This is a delicious fish dish that you can't help but love, and you'll enjoy the rich flavor of this amazing salmon. Even those that aren't partial to fish will find this recipe entirely enjoyable, and it's one of the best anti inflammatory recipes that you can prepare!

Ingredients:

For this dish, you will need:
1 pound of salmon
4 cloves of garlic
Fresh dill
1 lemon
3 green onions
Salt and pepper, as desired

Preparation:

To begin, turn the oven to 425 F, and let it heat as you go about preparing the fish.

Slice the salmon into steaks, ensuring that they're neither too thick nor too thin. Spray some cooking spray on aluminum foil, and place the salmon steaks onto the foil.

Sprinkle a bit of salt and black pepper onto the fish, as your taste demands. Dice the garlic and the onions very fine, and add a bit of the aromatics into the foil with the fish. Slice the lemon, and place one or two thin slices on each piece of fish. Add the fresh dill -- chopped, of course -- as the final touch.

Once the fish has been seasoned, use a piece of tin foil to cover the top of the fish - wrapping it tightly to ensure that the juices will not leak out. Place the wrapped fish steaks in a baking tray, and place the tray in the oven.

The salmon should take about 20 to 30 minutes to cook, and you can check to see that the salmon is done by pressing on the steaks with a fork. If it flakes easily, they're ready to eat.

Salmon Ceviche

This recipe comes from South America, specifically Peru - the land of the Incas. It's a unique dish that will surprise you, and it's an absolutely fantastic one when it's made right.

Ingredients:

For this dish, you will need:

1 pound of sushi-grade salmon (it is fresh enough to eat raw)
¼ tablespoon of natural brown sugar
Salt
Chili sauce
3 Limes
Black pepper
Cumin
Olive oil
2 cloves of garlic
1 small red onion
1 tomato
Fresh cilantro
1 avocado

Preparation:

To begin, add the brown sugar into a bowl with ½ teaspoon of chili sauce and 2 tablespoons of salt. Stir well, adding the juice from the three limes into the bowl. Add ¼ teaspoon each of cumin and black pepper, along with the same amount of olive oil.

Dice the garlic and the onion very fine, and stir them into the bowl. Dice the tomatoes and the cilantro, and add them into the mix. Cut the salmon into bite-sized cubes, and stir the salmon gently into the other ingredients.

The salmon will need to sit in the fridge overnight, though you can eat it after about 4 to 6 hours. Drain the liquid from the salmon, cut the avocado into cubes, add the cubes into the mix, and serve the delicious fish dish cold with whole wheat crackers.

Mixed Veggie Salad

If you want to keep cool during the summer, this delicious salad will definitely be the ideal dish for you! It will be a refreshing veggie dish that will go well with any meal, or you can even make a hearty main dish out of it by adding fish or chicken.

Ingredients:

For this dish, you will need:
1 head of lettuce
1 tomato
1 red onion
1 ear of corn
1 cucumber
1 head of cabbage
1 bunch of spinach

Preparation:

To begin, place the spinach and lettuce in a bowl to soak. Make sure to wash the spinach well, as you want to get all of the dirt out from among the leaves.

Dice the tomato into cubes, and place them in a bowl. Slice the onion into rings, and add them into the bowl as well.

Place a stock pot on the stove to heat, and add the ear of corn into the pot with 2 cups of water. Bring the water to a boil, and cook the corn until you're sure that it's properly tender. Use a knife to cut the kernels from the ear, and add the kernels into the salad.

Slice the cabbage very finely, and do the same for the lettuce. Cut the spinach into thin strips, and add the three leafy vegetables into the salad.

Cut the cucumber in half, and scoop out the majority of the slightly bitter seeds from inside. Slice the cucumber into small pieces, and add them into the salad. Toss the salad well, and add the dressing of your choice for a refreshing mixed vegetable delight!

Grilled Chicken Cranberry Spinach Salad

If you want a hearty salad that will be very filling, this is the one for you for! You'll be able to get all of the nutrients that you need, and without eating any simple carbs or refined foods. Just from the salad, you'll be filling your body with all the healthy nutrients that will keep it running!

Ingredients:

For this dish, you will need:

1 large chicken breast
1 bunch of spinach
½ cup of cranberries
½ cup of nuts (pecans, almonds, etc.)
¼ cup of poppy seeds
½ red onion
¼ cup of white wine vinegar
¼ cup of apple cider vinegar
¼ cup of peanut or olive oil
Salt and black pepper, to taste

Preparation:

To begin, slice the chicken breast into medium sized

pieces. You should get about 12 pieces from the chicken breast.

Place a skillet on the stove, and cook the chicken with a tablespoon of olive oil in the bottom of the pan. Make sure that the chicken's juices run clear, and remove them from the pan to cool in a plate on the side.

Slice the spinach, or use your hands to rip it apart. Add the cranberries, nuts, and poppy seeds into the bowl, and toss the salad.

Dice the red onion very finely, or run it through your blender. Mix the vinegars and the oil together, and use them to dress the salad. Toss the salad gently, and top with the grilled chicken breast.

Delicious Cucumber Salad

This salad will be an absolute delight, and you'll find that it will be one of the most enjoyable salads that you can eat while on the anti inflammatory diet. It's easy to make, and it requires very few ingredients to prepare.

Ingredients:

For this dish, you will need:

2 cucumbers
3 tomatoes
1 red onion
Mayonnaise
White vinegar
Salt and black pepper, to taste
Dill

Preparation:

To begin, slice the cucumbers in half. Cut the halved cucumbers into slivers, making sure that they are thin enough to eat easily. (Note: The peel on some cucumbers will be very bitter, so peel them if necessary.) Cut the tomatoes into slivers as well, and add them into the bowl with the cucumbers. Cut the onion into thin rings, and stir them in with the cucumbers.

In a separate bowl, combine 3 tablespoons of vinegar with a tablespoon of white vinegar. Add salt and pepper as desired, and mix the dressing in with the vegetables.

Tofu Salad

If you're a tofu lover, this is definitely the salad for you! It's loaded with all the healthy nutrients your body needs, and you'll find that it will be a surprisingly filling side dish despite the fact that it's mostly made with vegetables.

Ingredients:

For this dish, you will need:
1 package of firm Tofu
Korean sweet chili sauce
Ginger root
2 cloves of garlic
Soy sauce
Sesame oil
1 cup of snow peas
2 carrots
1 head of red cabbage
1 cup of peanuts

Preparation:

To begin, combine the chili sauce with a tablespoon each of soy sauce and sesame oil in a bowl. Dice the garlic until it's very fine, and crush the ginger. Add both of the aromatics into the sauce, and stir well. Cut the tofu into cubes, and add it into the sauce. Place the mixture into the fridge, and let it marinate in the cool fridge for about an hour.

Place a pot of water on the stove to heat, and leave the pot on high heat until the water is boiling. Turn the water to medium heat, and drop the snow peas into the water. Let them sit for about 3 minutes, and scoop them out with a slotted spoon. Place them in a bowl of cold water to cool off for a few minutes, and drain them before setting them aside.

Slice the cabbage very finely, and use the grater to grate the carrots into long, thin strips. Chop the peanuts as much as you can.

Add the carrots into the bowl with the cabbage, and add the snow peas as well. Toss the vegetables to mix them, and add the dressing with the tofu to complete the flavor. Garnish the salad with peanuts, and serve.

Tofu Scramble

If scrambled eggs in the morning aren't your thing, you may find that this delicious tofu scramble will be your best option! It's a vegetarian's dream, and it's a delightfully low fat meal that you can enjoy at any time of the day!

Ingredients:

For this dish, you will need:
1 pack of firm silken tofu
Olive oil
1 onion
4 cloves of garlic
1 green bell pepper
2 potatoes
2 green tomatoes
Salt

Preparation:

To begin, peel the potatoes and cut them into bite-sized pieces. Place them in a pot on the stove, along with enough water to cover the potatoes. Turn the heat on high, and bring the potatoes to a boil. Cook them until they are just soft enough to spear them with a fork, and remove them from the heat.

In a skillet, place a tablespoon of olive oil. Dice the garlic very fine, and add it into the bottom of the skillet. Once the garlic has turned slightly golden brown, add the potatoes into the skillet. Cook them until the potatoes are properly tender, and remove them from the pan.

Place the skillet back on the stove, along with two tablespoons of olive oil. Dice the onions as the oil is heating, and add them into the skillet to cook. Once the onion has become tender and slightly transparent, add the green bell pepper -- which you will have de-seeded and diced. Cook until the bell pepper is soft.

Dice the green tomatoes, and add them into the skillet. Cook them until they begin to release their juices, and add the salt as desired. Add the potatoes into the mix, and cook for a few more minutes.

Once the potatoes are properly coated with the juices of the tomatoes, add the tofu into the pan. You will need to mash it using a masher or a fork, as that will make it much easier for you to scramble. Mix the tofu in with the rest of the ingredients, and let it cook until it gets nice and hot.

Serve with bran muffins or whole wheat toast

Baked Tofu

This is a dish that you'd never expect to enjoy, but it's surprisingly enjoyable! Even if you aren't a tofu enthusiast, it's very likely that you'll love the taste of this dish. It may take time to get used to, but it's a healthy meal that will grow on you with time.

Ingredients:

For this dish, you will need:
1 pack of firm tofu
Soy sauce
Sesame seeds
Ginger
Honey
1 cup of brown rice
Water

Preparation:

The night before you are going to eat the dish, crush the ginger and add it into a bowl with 3 tablespoons of soy sauce. Remove the tofu from the package, and drain it thoroughly before putting it into a Ziploc plastic bag. Pour the soy sauce mixture into the bag, and shake it to coat the tofu. Place it in the fridge to marinate overnight. In the morning, turn the tofu over to allow the other side to marinate properly.

Place the brown rice in a pot with 2 ½ cups of water, and cover the rice with a lid once the water has begun to boil. It will take the rice about 45 minutes to cook completely, and you may have to add a bit more water to ensure that it doesn't burn.

As the rice is cooking, toast the sesame seeds in a pan. Keep the fire on low heat, and add about ½ cup of the seeds into the pan once it is already hot. It will take about three minutes to toast the seeds.

Once the seeds have been toasted, let them cool off on a plate, and sprinkle the cool seeds onto the tofu once you have removed it from the plastic bag. Preheat the oven to about 350 F, and place the tofu into the oven to bake for about 8 minutes once it has heated properly. Make sure to pour the remaining marinade over the tofu, and serve the baked tofu on a bed of rice -- sprinkled with the rest of the seeds.

Lime and Cilantro Tofu

This is a unique Tofu-rich twist on a classic Latin American dish, and you'll find that it has all the great taste that you've come to expect from Mexican and South American food. It's a rich dish that will set your mouth watering immediately.

Ingredients:

For this dish, you will need:
1 pack of extra firm tofu
Cilantro
4 cloves of garlic
2 limes
Soy sauce
Cumin
Natural brown sugar
Cayenne pepper
Olive oil

Preparation:

To begin, dice fresh cilantro until you have about a handful of the green stuff - or ¼ cup. Dice the garlic very finely, and add it into a bowl with the cilantro. Grate the zest from the 2 limes, and add it into the bowl with the garlic. Squeeze the lemon juice, and add it into the bowl as well. Add in a teaspoon and a half of soy sauce, a teaspoon of the cumin, half a teaspoon of brown sugar, and half a teaspoon of cayenne pepper. Pour in about a tablespoon of olive oil, and mix all of the ingredients together well.

Open the package of tofu, drain the liquid, and add the large cube of extra firm tofu into a Ziploc plastic bag. Pour the marinade into the bag, and shake the tofu gently to coat it with the liquid. Once it has been properly coated, place it in the fridge to marinate. You can leave it overnight if you want, or it will be good to eat in about an hour.

Once the marinating is done, remove the tofu from the bag - using a slotted spoon to allow the liquid to drain off the tofu.

Place a skillet on the stove to heat, and add a tablespoon of olive oil into the bottom of the pan. Place the marinated tofu in the skillet, and cook it until it has been evenly browned on all sides. Apply the marinade each time you flip the tofu, and that will ensure that it absorbs all of the delicious flavor. It will take about 15 minutes to cook, and you can serve the cooked tofu on a bed of brown rice.

Tofu Watercress Salad

This delicious salad will be the perfect side dish for a hearty meal, or it will help you to stay faithful to your diet. It's a very low fat and low calorie dish, but it's loaded with the healthy nutrients that your body needs!

Ingredients:

For this dish, you will need:
Bean sprouts
1 pack of firm tofu
2 cans of tuna
2 tomatoes
1 bunch of watercress
Pickled radish
½ red onion
4 cloves of garlic
Sesame oil
Soy sauce

Preparation:

To begin, pull out a baking dish to prepare the salad in. Cover the bottom of the tray with bean sprouts, and follow it with a layer of tofu. Drain the tofu and slice it into thin pieces to lay on top of the bean sprouts. Open the cans of tuna, drain the liquid, and layer the tuna on top of the tofu.

Cut the watercress into strips, and add a layer on top of the tuna. Dice the tomatoes into small cubes, and use them to make the next layer of the salad. The top layer will be the Japanese pickled radish, and you can use as much of that as you like.

Dice the onion very fine, and place it in a bowl. Place a skillet on the stove to heat, and add a tablespoon of sesame oil into the bottom. Dice the garlic, and add it into the skillet to cook. Make sure the garlic has browned properly, and use a spoon to scoop the garlic pieces from the skillet. Add the onions into the skillet to cook, and cook them until they too are browned.

Add the garlic pieces into the salad on top of the radish, and cover the salad with the sesame oil and the cooked onions. Add half a cup of soy sauce into the salad, and stir it well to mix everything together. Serve with crackers, or as a stand alone dish.

Fruit Salad

This delicious fruit salad will get your body going in the morning, or it will be the perfect dessert to enjoy after a hearty meal. The best thing about it is that it's 100% natural and healthy, so you can have it anytime and anywhere!

Ingredients:

For this dish, you will need:
Strawberries
1 red apple
1 green apple
Berries (blueberries, raspberries, etc.)
2 kiwi fruits
½ pineapple
Grapes

Preparation:

To begin, cut the stalk from the top of the strawberries. Cut the strawberries in half, and add them into a bowl.

Cut the red apple in half, and use your knife to remove the core. Cut the halves into thirds, and cut each of the resulting slices into bite-sized pieces. Repeat the same process with the green apple.

Place the berries into a colander, and run cold water over them. Raspberries can be damaged if the pressure of the water from the sink is too high, so make sure the water is gentle.

Cut the core out of the pineapple, and cut the rest into slices. Each round slice can be cut into eight pieces, and add the pieces into the bowl with the strawberries, apples, and berries.

Peel the kiwi fruit with a paring knife, and cut the ends off of the fruit. Cut the kiwi into slices, and cut each slice into quarters before adding them into the bowl.

Run the grapes under cold water, and drain them thoroughly. Cut them in half, and add the halves of the grapes into the bowl with the rest of the fruits.

Garnish with a bit of wheat germ, a sprinkling of natural brown sugar, and enjoy!

Healthy Oatmeal

If you want to start the day out with a meal that will be very enjoyable as well as filling, this is the breakfast for you. It's quick and easy to make, and you'll have no problem eating it while on the anti inflammatory diet!

Ingredients:

For this dish, you will need:

1 cup of steel cut oats
3 cups of water
1 cup of almond milk
½ cup of assorted nuts
½ cup of raisins and cranberries
Flaked coconut
Cinnamon
Vanilla
Honey

Preparation:

To begin, place a pot on the stove, and add the three cups of water into the pot. Add a pinch of salt, and bring the water to a rolling boil. Once the water has begun to boil, drop the oats into the water. Cook them for about

20 minutes, or until soft. (The steel cut oats will get soft very quickly, so keep an eye on them.)
Once the oats have cooked properly, remove them from the fire. Add the milk into the oats, and stir in the cranberries and raisins.

Use a knife to chop the nuts, and add them into the oats as well. Add a tablespoon of the flaked coconuts, and stir 2 teaspoons of vanilla extract into the oatmeal. Add two tablespoons of honey to make the oatmeal sweet, and add a pinch or two of cinnamon.

Return the pot with the oatmeal to the fire, and turn the fire on low. You will need to stir the oatmeal continuously, mixing the oats with the milk and the other ingredients. Don't let the oatmeal burn, but just leave it on the stove long enough to heat up the **oatmeal** once the oats have been added.

Serve with a sprinkling of wheat germ, sesame seeds, and amaranth seeds to make your oatmeal healthy and filling!

Banana Nut Breakfast Cereal

This is a meal that is guaranteed to keep you healthy, and you'll find that it's one of the tastiest breakfasts that you can eat. It will be loaded with nutrients, and you will definitely enjoy it once you get used to its unique, varied flavor.

Ingredients:

For this dish, you will need:

Water
1 cup of almond milk
Quinoa
1 banana
Oats
Oat bran
Cinnamon
Salt, for flavor
Assorted nuts
Brown sugar
Vanilla extract

Preparation:

To begin, place a sauce pan on the stove to heat. Add a

tablespoon of quinoa into the pan, along with ½ a cup of almond milk and a few tablespoons of water. Once the mixture has begun to boil, turn the heat down to its lowest setting.

Let the oatmeal mixture simmer for about 5 minutes, and test frequently to ensure that the quinoa is getting soft. Once the quinoa is soft, add the banana into the pan. Use a fork to mash it, and stir it in with the quinoa.

As the banana is cooking with the quinoa, add a tablespoon each of oats and oat bran. The mixture should get thicker very quickly, and it's the sign that the ingredients are cooking properly. You will need to keep it cooking on very low heat for about 5 more minutes, though stir it gently to ensure that it doesn't burn.

Once the mixture has thickened, add a tablespoon of brown sugar, a teaspoon of vanilla extract, and a pinch of salt and cinnamon each. Chop the walnuts into small pieces, and add them into the cereal to give it the delicious nutty flavor that makes it the perfect breakfast!

All of these recipes can be found online, though some of them are our own original creations. You can probably find similar recipes on websites like AllRecpes.com,

About.com, and particularly ElanasPantry.com. They are all recipes that someone made, and we just wanted to share them with you. We've made a few adjustments to the various recipes so that you'll get only our unique grain-free flavor on the recipes, but you'll find that there are many like them. The important thing is that you can enjoy your grain-free cooking and eating, and we wanted to provide you with a recipe book that you can use to prepare delicious meals free of grain and gluten. We apologize if you've seen these recipes elsewhere, and we hope that you enjoy the creations we have presented to you!

NEW CONTENT FOR SECOND EDITION

Arugula Salad

This makes a great light lunch or goes really well with supper as a side dish. Makes 4 servings.

What You'll Need:

4 cups of arugula leaves (young, rinsed, dry)
1 avocado (peeled, pitted, sliced)
1 cup of tomatoes (cherry, halves)
1/4 cup of onions (sweet red, chopped)
1/4 cup of Parmesan cheese (grated)
1/4 cup of pine nuts
2 tablespoons of olive oil
1 tablespoon of rice vinegar
Salt and pepper

How to Make It:

Mix the 2 tablespoons of olive oil, 1 tablespoon of rice vinegar, and dashes of salt and pepper in a cup with a whisk. In a large salad bowl combine the 4 cups of arugula leaves (young, rinsed, dry), 1 avocado (peeled, pitted, sliced), 1 cup of tomatoes (cherry, halves), 1/4 cup of onions (sweet red, chopped), 1/4 cup of Parmesan cheese (grated), and 1/4 cup of pine nuts by tossing. Drizzle the seasoned oil and vinegar and serve immediately.

Artichoke and Chicken Pasta

This savory chicken pasta meal goes well with steamed vegetables and a nice crisp salad. It also makes for a nice lunch. Make 6 servings.

What You'll Need:

1 lb of pasta (uncooked, whole grain)
1 lb of chicken breasts (boneless, skinless, cut into bite-size)
2 lemons (wedges)
1 can of artichoke hearts (14 oz, marinated, drained, chopped)
1 tomato (chopped)
1/2 cup of feta cheese (crumbled)
1/2 cup of onions (chopped)
3 tablespoons of parsley (fresh chopped)
2 tablespoons of lemon juice
1 tablespoon of olive oil
2 teaspoons of oregano (dried)
1 teaspoon of garlic (minced)
Salt and pepper
Water

How to Make It:
Prep: Cook the pound of pasta according to package

directions.

Add the tablespoon of olive oil to a skillet and turn to medium high heat. Sauté the 1/2 cup of chopped onions and the teaspoon of minced garlic for a couple of minutes. Add the pound of boneless, skinless, chopped chicken breasts and cook until the chicken turns white, about 5 minutes. Turn the heat to medium low and stir in the cooked pasta along with the 1 can of artichoke hearts (14 oz, marinated, drained, chopped), 1 tomato (chopped), 1/2 cup of feta cheese (crumbled), 1/2 cup of onions (chopped), 3 tablespoons of parsley (fresh chopped), 2 tablespoons of lemon juice, 1 tablespoon of olive oil, 2 teaspoons of oregano (dried), 1 teaspoon of garlic (minced), and dashes of salt and pepper. Stir until the mixture is hot, a couple of minutes. Add lemon wedges to the servings on the plate for garnishment.

Baked Flounder

This dish is so delicious, filled with vegetables and seasonings over the baked flounder. Makes 4 servings.

What You'll Need:

1 pound of flounder fillets
24 kalamata olives (pitted, chopped)
12 basil leaves (fresh chopped, divided)
5 tomatoes (roma)
1/4 cup of onions (chopped)
1/4 cup of white grape juice
4 tablespoons of capers
3 tablespoons of Parmesan cheese (grated)
2 tablespoons of olive oil (extra virgin)
1 teaspoon of garlic (minced)
1 teaspoon of lemon juice
Italian seasoning
Water

How to Make It:

Prep: Preheat the oven to 425 degrees Fahrenheit.

Add water to a medium saucepan and turn to high to bring to a boil. Add the 5 roma tomatoes, then remove and place the tomatoes in a bowl of ice water. Drain the water and skin the tomatoes, chop, and set to the side. Meanwhile, pour the 2 tablespoons of extra virgin olive oil in a skillet and turn to medium heat. Add the 1/4 cup of chopped onions and sauté. Add the teaspoon of minced garlic along with a couple of dashes of Italian seasoning and stir. Add the chopped skinned tomatoes and cook until heated. Add 6 of the fresh chopped basil leaves with the 1/4 cup of white grape juice, 4 tablespoons of capers, and 1 teaspoon of lemon juice and stir. Turn the heat to low and add the 3 tablespoons of Parmesan cheese and cook for another 15 minutes. Place the pound of flounder fillets in a shallow baking dish. Pour the sauce over the top. Set the remaining 6 fresh chopped basil leaves on top of the sauce. Bake in the hot oven for 12 minutes. Serve immediately.

Black Bean Hummus

We love many hummus recipes, this one is different because it is made with black beans instead of the usual garbanzo beans. Enjoy with your choice of chips or crackers. Makes 8 servings.

What You'll Need:

1 can of black beans (15 oz, drain but reserve 2 tablespoons of the liquid)
10 Greek olives
2 tablespoons of lemon juice
1 1/2 tablespoons of tahini
3/4 teaspoon of cumin (ground)
1/2 teaspoon of garlic
1/4 teaspoon of cayenne pepper
1/4 teaspoon of paprika
Salt and pepper

How to Make It:

Add the 1 can of black beans (15 oz, drain but reserve 2 tablespoons of the liquid), 2 tablespoons of lemon juice, 1 1/2 tablespoons of tahini, 3/4 teaspoon of cumin (ground), 1/2 teaspoon of garlic, 1/4 teaspoon of cayenne pepper, and dashes of salt and pepper to a blender or food processor and blend until smooth. Scrape into a serving dish and arrange the 10 Greek olives around the top and sprinkle the 1/4 teaspoon of paprika over all.

Broccoli and Shells Skillet

This is a quick serve side dish that is savory and goes great with chicken or beef or fish. Makes 6 servings.

What You'll Need:

1 1/2 heads of broccoli (florets)
5 cups of pasta shells (cooked, whole grain)
1/4 cup of olive oil
1 tablespoon of Parmesan cheese (grated)
3/4 teaspoon of garlic (minced)
1/2 teaspoon of red pepper flakes (crushed)
Salt and pepper
Pot of boiling water

How to Make It:

Cook the 1 1/2 head of broccoli florets in a pot of boiling water for 5 minutes. Remove, drain, and set aside in a colander. Add the 1/4 cup of olive oil to a large skillet and turn to medium heat. Stir in the 3/4 teaspoon of minced garlic and saute for a couple of minutes. Stir in the broccoli and cook for another 10 minutes. Toss in the cooked pasta shells and add the 1/2 teaspoon of crushed red pepper flakes and several dashes of salt and pepper. Sprinkle with the tablespoon of grated

Parmesan cheese before serving.

Chilled Tomato Soup

This is a very healthy soup because all the ingredients are raw, with exception of the navy beans. This is a great light lunch as well. Makes 8 servings.

What You'll Need:

5 scallions (chopped)
3 tomatoes (diced)
1 can of tomato juice (46 oz)
1 English cucumber (diced)
2 1/2 cups of navy beans (canned, drained, rinsed)
1 cup of bell pepper (green, diced)
2/3 cup of celery (diced)
6 tablespoons of balsamic vinegar
2 tablespoons of olive oil
1 tablespoons of basil (fresh minced)
1 tablespoon of parsley (fresh minced)
1/2 tablespoon of oregano (fresh minced)
1 teaspoon of cumin (ground)
1 teaspoon of garlic (minced)
Salt and pepper

How to Make It:

Very simple, just combine the 5 scallions (chopped), 3

tomatoes (diced), 1 can of tomato juice (46 oz), 1 English cucumber (diced), 2 1/2 cups of navy beans (canned, drained, rinsed), 1 cup of bell pepper (green, diced), 2/3 cup of celery (diced), 6 tablespoons of balsamic vinegar, 2 tablespoons of olive oil, 1 tablespoons of basil (fresh minced), 1 tablespoon of parsley (fresh minced), 1/2 tablespoon of oregano (fresh minced), 1 teaspoon of cumin (ground), 1 teaspoon of garlic (minced), and several dashes of salt and pepper in a large bowl or soup tureen. Place in the refrigerator for several hours before serving.

Garbanzo Bean Humus

This is a delicious appetizer or snack, tastes great with pita chips. Makes about 2 1/2 cups.

What You'll Need:

1 can of garbanzo beans (15 oz, drain but reserve half of the liquid)
4 tablespoons of lemon juice
2 tablespoons of olive oil
2 tablespoons of tahini
1 teaspoon of garlic (minced)
Salt and pepper

How to Make It:

Add the 1 can of garbanzo beans (15 oz, half drained, use half the liquid), 4 tablespoons of lemon juice, 2 tablespoons of tahini, 1 teaspoon of garlic (minced), and dashes of salt and pepper into a blender or food processor. Blend until smooth and "dip" consistency. Scrape into a serving dish and pour the 2 tablespoons of olive oil over the top.

Italian Chicken and Cherry Peppers

This is a delicious main dish meal complete with chicken breasts, Italian turkey sausage, savory herbs, artichoke hearts, and cherry peppers. Makes 6 servings.

What You'll Need:

6 chicken breasts halves (boneless, skinless)
1/2 pound of Italian turkey sausage
18 cherry peppers
1 can of artichoke hearts (14 oz, drained, chopped)
2 cups of chicken stock
1 cup of pepperoncini peppers (sliced, in liquid)
1/2 cup of olives (pitted Kalamata)
1/2 cup of onions (sliced)
2 tablespoons of olive oil
1 tablespoon of basil (fresh chopped)
1 tablespoons of herbes de Provence
1 tablespoon of marjoram (fresh chopped)
1 tablespoon of oregano (fresh chopped)
2 teaspoons of cumin (ground)
2 teaspoons of garlic (minced)
1/2 teaspoon of red pepper flakes (crushed)
Salt and pepper

How to Make It:

Prep: Preheat the oven to 350 degrees Fahrenheit.

Sprinkle salt and pepper over the 6 chicken breasts halves. Sprinkle on the 2 teaspoons of ground cumin. Set aside. Pour the 2 tablespoons of olive oil into a Dutch oven and turn to medium high heat. Place the 6 seasoned chicken breast halves in the hot oil for about 5 minutes until brown on bottom, turn over the continue cooking for another minute. Take the chicken breasts out and set aside.
Add the 1/2 cup of onions (sliced) into the Dutch oven and a couple dashes of salt and sauté for five minutes. Turn the heat to medium low and add the 1 tablespoon of herbes de Provence, 2 teaspoons of garlic (minced), and the 1/2 teaspoon of red pepper flakes (crushed). Pour in the 1 cup of pepperoncini peppers (sliced, in liquid), cook, and stir for another couple of minutes. Place the slightly cooked chicken breast halves on top of the onions and herbs. Pour the 2 cups of chicken stock over the chicken. Stuff all the cherry peppers with the Italian turkey sausage. Add the stuffed cherry peppers along with the 14 oz can of drained artichoke hearts and 1/2 cup of olives (pitted Kalamata) to the Dutch oven. Turn the heat back up to medium high, cover, and let cook for 60 more minutes.   Prior to serving sprinkle the 1 tablespoon of basil (fresh chopped), 1 tablespoon of

marjoram (fresh chopped), and 1 tablespoon of oregano (fresh chopped) over the top.

Mediterranean Fish Packets

These are delicious little packets of seasoned halibut with onions, olives, tomatoes, and capers. Makes 4 servings.

What You'll Need:

4 halibut fillets
1 jar of olives (5 oz, kalamata, pitted)
1 tomato (chopped)
1/2 cup of onion (chopped)
1/4 cup of capers
1 tablespoon of Greek seasoning
1 tablespoon of lemon juice
Salt and pepper

How to Make It:

Prep: Preheat the oven to 350 degrees Fahrenheit.

Pull off 4 sheets of heavy duty foil. Place a halibut fillet on each one. Sprinkle with the tablespoon of Greek seasoning. In a bowl, combine the 1 jar of olives (5 oz, kalamata, pitted), 1 tomato (chopped), 1/2 cup of onion (chopped), 1/4 cup of capers, 1 tablespoon of Greek seasoning, 1 tablespoon of lemon juice, and dashes of salt and pepper. Divide over the 4 halibut fillets. Seal the edges of the foil to create packets. Bake for about 35 minutes.

Mediterranean Mackerel

Fish is highly nutritious containing Omega 3 fatty acids, which work to reduce inflammation in the body. Makes 6 servings.

What You'll Need:

6 mackerel fillets
1/4 cup of olive oil
Paprika
Salt and pepper
Lemon slices

How to Make It:

Prep: Preheat the broiler. Bring the top rack to the highest level. Spray a baking pan with cooking spray.

First, take the 1/4 cup of olive oil and rub both sides of the 6 mackerel fillets. Set them on their skin on the baking pan. Sprinkle each one with paprika, salt and pepper. Place 2 or 3 lemon slices on top of each mackerel. Bake for about 6 minutes under the broiler and then serve immediately.

Mediterranean Style Baked Potatoes

Olive oil and lemon makes these into a nutritious side dish. Makes 4 servings.

What You'll Need:

6 cups of potatoes (quartered pieces, peeled)
1 1/2 cups of chicken stock
1/3 cup of olive oil
1/4 cup of lemon juice
1 teaspoon of garlic (minced)
1 teaspoon of rosemary (dried)
1 teaspoon of thyme (dried)
Salt and pepper

How to Make It:

Prep: Preheat the oven to 350 degrees Fahrenheit.

Combine the 1 1/2 cups of chicken stock, 1/3 cup of olive oil, 1/4 cup of lemon juice, 1 teaspoon of garlic (minced), 1 teaspoon of rosemary (dried), 1 teaspoon of thyme (dried), and dashes of salt and pepper in a bowl with a whisk. Place the potatoes in a 2 quart baking dish. Pour the liquid over the top. Cover with foil and bake in the hot oven for 2 hours, stirring at one hour.

Mushroom Omelet

This makes for a delicious breakfast filled with the goodness of a tasty Portobello mushroom. Have this for a delicious breakfast or for a meal any time of day. Makes 4 servings.

What You'll Need:

8 eggs
4 Portobello mushrooms caps (sliced)
1 cup of mozzarella cheese (shredded)
1 cup of onion (chopped)
1 1/4 tablespoon of olive oil
1 1/4 tablespoon of pesto
1 1/4 tablespoon of water
Salt and pepper

How to Make It:

Add the 1 1/4 tablespoon of olive oil to a skillet and turn to medium heat. Stir in the 4 Portobello mushrooms caps (sliced) and the 1 cup of onion (chopped) and cook for about 4 minutes. Divide the mushroom/onion mixture into fours. In a bowl, crack and beat the 8 eggs then combine with the 1 1/4 tablespoon of water. Add dashes of salt and pepper. Pour the 1/4 of the eggs into the hot skillet with 1/4 of the the mushrooms and onions. Allow the eggs to set, flip, sprinkle 1/4 cup of mozzarella cheese and 1/4 of the 1 1/4 tablespoon of pesto over the top and gently fold the egg over to make an omelet. Repeat 3 more times until all servings are cooked.

Roasted Asparagus Dish

This is a delicious asparagus dish with a different twist, with the addition of turkey ham and a fried egg. Makes 4 servings.

What You'll Need:

4 eggs
1 bunch of asparagus (trimmed)
1/4 cup of turkey ham (minced)
2 tablespoons of olive oil (divided)
1 tablespoon of lemon juice
1 tablespoon of lemon zest
1 teaspoon of vinegar (white distilled)
Salt and pepper
Water

How to Make It:

Prep: Preheat the oven to 425 degrees Fahrenheit. Drizzle 1 tablespoon of olive oil over the asparagus (laid in a single layer) in a baking dish, set aside.

Pour the remaining tablespoon of olive oil in a skillet and turn heat to medium low. Stir in the 1/4 cup of minced turkey ham and heat through about 3 minutes. Spread the cooked turkey ham over the asparagus. Sprinkle dashes of salt and pepper over the ham and vegetables. Bake in the hot oven for 10 minutes, flip the asparagus and toss the ham and cook for another 5 minutes. Meanwhile add a couple of inches of water to a large size saucepan and put on high heat. When the water boils pour in the 1 teaspoon of vinegar (white distilled) and a dash of salt and turn the heat to medium low. Crack 1 egg and put it in a small cup, then pour into the water, do this with each egg, separately, give the egg a second to set before adding the next. Leave in the water for 5 minutes, and then carefully remove the egg without tearing it. Place the eggs together on a plate near the heat of the stove. Sprinkle the 1 tablespoon of lemon juice and the 1 tablespoon of lemon zest over the asparagus. Add dashes of pepper on top. Divide the asparagus and turkey ham between 4 plates. Place one egg on top of the asparagus on each plate. Serve immediately.

Simple Tomato Salad

This salad just screams Mediterranean cuisine, but so flavorful and nutritious. Makes 6 servings.

What You'll Need:

4 tomatoes (large, red, thick sliced)
2 cups of mozzarella cheese (as many slices as there are tomato slices)
3 tablespoons of olive oil (extra virgin)
Basil leaves (one whole leaf for every tomato slice)
Salt and pepper

How to Make It:

Arrange the tomato slices divided equally on 6 salad plates (or all on a large platter). Place a slice of mozzarella cheese on top of each tomato slice. Place a fresh basil leaf on top of each mozzarella cheese slice. Drizzle the 3 tablespoons of extra virgin olive oil over the tops and season with dashes of salt and pepper.

Spanish Chicken and Rice

This is chicken and rice cooked in true Mediterranean style. Makes 6 servings.

What You'll Need:

6 chicken breast halves (boneless, skinless)
1/2 of a can of pineapples (20 oz can, chunked, drained but reserved juice)
1/2 of a can of tomatoes (14.5 oz, stewed)
1 1/8 cups of black olives
1/2 cup of bell pepper (red, thin sliced)
1/3 cup of salsa
1/4 cup of onions (chopped)
1 tablespoon of cornstarch
1 tablespoon of olive oil
1 tablespoon of water
1/2 teaspoon of cinnamon (ground)
1/2 teaspoon of cumin (ground)
3/4 teaspoon of garlic (minced)
Salt and pepper

How to Make It:

Place the 1/2 can of drained crushed pineapples in a bowl and sprinkle with salt. Add the tablespoon of olive oil to a large skillet and cook the 6 chicken breast halves (boneless, skinless). Sprinkle the 1/2 teaspoon of cinnamon (ground) and the 1/2 teaspoon of cumin (ground) over the chicken. Stir in the 1/4 cup of onions (chopped) and the 3/4 teaspoon of garlic (minced) and saute. Add the reserved pineapple juice along with the 1/2 of a can of tomatoes (14.5 oz, stewed), 1/3 cup of salsa, and the 1 1/8 cup of black olives and stir. Cover the skillet and turn to low and cook for 25 minutes. In a small cup mix the tablespoon of cornstarch with the tablespoon of water and pour into the skillet and stir. Add in the 1/2 cup of bell pepper (red, thin sliced) and the salted crushed pineapple. Sprinkle with salt and pepper and heat the pineapple and bell pepper.

Spanish Tapas

This is a delicious dish with avocado halves filled with delicious tuna and just the right amount of seasonings. Makes 4 servings.

What You'll Need:

3 scallions (sliced thin)
2 avocados (ripe, halved, pitted)
1 can of tuna (12 oz, packed in water, drained)
1/4 cup of bell pepper (red, chopped)
1 tablespoon of mayonnaise
Balsamic vinegar
Salt and pepper

How to Make It:

Combine the 3 scallions (sliced thin), 1 can of tuna (12 oz, packed in water, drained), 1/4 cup of bell pepper (red, chopped), 1 tablespoon of mayonnaise, a dash of balsamic vinegar, and a couple dashes of salt and pepper in a bowl. Equally divide the tuna into each avocado half. Serve immediately.

Spicy Hummus

Sometimes you want your hummus with a little kick, try this spiced with roasted red peppers. Makes 8 servings.

What You'll Need:

1 can of garbanzo beans (15 oz, drained)
1 jar of roasted red peppers (4 oz)
3 tablespoons of lemon juice
1 tablespoon of parsley (fresh chopped)
1 1/2 tablespoons of tahini
1/2 teaspoon of cayenne pepper
1/2 teaspoon of cumin (ground)
1/2 teaspoon of garlic (minced)
Salt and pepper

How to Make It:

Add 1 can of garbanzo beans (15 oz, drained), 1 jar of roasted red peppers (4 oz), 3 tablespoons of lemon juice, 1 1/2 tablespoons of tahini, 1/2 teaspoon of cayenne pepper, 1/2 teaspoon of cumin (ground), 1/2 teaspoon of garlic (minced), and dashes of salt and pepper to a blender or food processor and blend until smooth. Scrape into a serving dish and sprinkle the 1 tablespoon of parsley (fresh chopped) over the top.

Tomato and Couscous Salad

This is a delicious salad filled with delicious fresh vegetables and herbs coupled with couscous. Makes 6 servings.

What You'll Need:

2 heirloom tomatoes (quartered)
8 cherry tomatoes (quartered)
1/2 of an English cucumber (diced)
1 cups of vegetable stock
1/2 cup of couscous
1/2 cup of feta cheese (crumbled)
1/4 cup of basil (fresh leaves, packed)
1/4 cup of olives (pitted green)
1/4 cup of olive oil (extra virgin + 1 tablespoon)
1/8 cup of onions (sliced thin)
1/8 cup of parsley (fresh, flat leaf)
1/8 cup of vinegar (white balsamic)
1 tablespoons of lemon juice
1/2 tablespoon of oregano (fresh chopped)
1/2 tablespoon of thyme (fresh chopped)
1/4 teaspoon of garlic (minced)

How to Make It:

Pour the cup of vegetable stock into a saucepan and turn to medium heat. Place a skillet on medium heat and add the tablespoon of extra virgin olive oil. Add the 1/2 cup of couscous and cook for 10 minutes, stirring often, to brown. Add the toasted couscous to the hot vegetable stock and turn to low. Cover and simmer until the liquid absorbs for another 15 minutes. Pour the couscous and stock into a large bowl, tossing with a fork. Set aside to cool. Add the 1/4 cup of basil (fresh leaves, packed), 1/4 cup of olives (pitted green), 1/8 cup of parsley (fresh, flat leaf), 1/2 tablespoon of oregano (fresh chopped), 1/2 tablespoon of thyme (fresh chopped), and 1/4 teaspoon of garlic (minced) into a blender or food processor and combine until rough chopped. Add the herbs to the couscous, tossing to combine. Add the 2 heirloom tomatoes (quartered), 8 cherry tomatoes (quartered), 1/2 of an English cucumber (diced), 1/2 cup of feta cheese (crumbled), and 1/8 cup of onions (sliced thin) and toss. In a small bowl combine the 1/4 cup of olive oil (extra virgin), /8 cup of vinegar (white balsamic) and the 1 tablespoons of lemon juice with a whisk. Drizzle over the couscous and tomato salad and toss to coat. Serve immediately.

White Bean Soup

This is a filling meal, makes a great lunch or a nice course with supper. Makes 4 servings.

What You'll Need:

2 cans of white kidney beans (16 oz, drained, rinsed)
1 bunch of spinach (rinsed, chopped fine)
2 cups of water
1 1/2 cups of chicken stock
1/2 cup of celery (chopped)
1/2 cup of onion (chopped)
1 tablespoon of lemon juice
1 tablespoon of olive oil
1/2 teaspoon of garlic (minced)
1/8 teaspoon of thyme (dried)
Salt and pepper
Parmesan cheese (grated)

How to Make It:

Pour the tablespoon of olive oil in a large saucepan and turn to medium high heat. Sauté the 1/2 cup of celery (chopped) and the 1/2 cup of onion (chopped) for about 6 minutes. Stir in the 1/2 teaspoon of minced garlic. Add the 2 cans of white kidney beans (16 oz, drained, rinsed), 2 cups of water, 1 1/2 cups of chicken stock, 1/8 teaspoon of thyme (dried), and dashes of salt and pepper. Reserve 2 cups of strained beans and vegetables, put the rest in a food processor or blender, and blend until creamy. Add back to the pot with the reserved beans and vegetables. Turn the heat to high and bring to a boil, stirring often. Add the 1 bunch of spinach (rinsed, chopped fine) and boil for another minute. Turn off the heat and stir in the tablespoon of lemon juice. Ladle into bowls and garnish with Parmesan cheese.

Printed in Great Britain
by Amazon.co.uk, Ltd.,
Marston Gate.